GRAHAM HARVEY

Who's Who
in
The Archers

2012

BBC
BOOKS

1 3 5 7 9 10 8 6 4 2

This book is published to accompany the BBC Radio 4 serial *The Archers*.
The editor of *The Archers* is Vanessa Whitburn.

Published in 2011 by BBC Books, an imprint of Ebury Publishing.
A Random House Group Company.

Main text by Graham Harvey
Copyright © Woodlands Books Ltd 2011

The Random House Group Limited Reg. No. 954009.
Addresses for companies within the Random House Group can be found
at www.randomhouse.co.uk

A CIP catalogue record for this book is available from the British Library.

ISBN 978 1 849 90242 7

Commissioning editor: Albert DePetrillo
Editorial manager: Nicholas Payne
Project editor: Steve Tribe

Printed and bound in Great Britain by CPI Group (UK) Ltd, Croydon, CR0 4YY

Events in Ambridge are constantly changing, but we have done our
best to make *Who's Who in The Archers 2012* accurate at the time of
publication. Official Archers Website: bbc.co.uk/archers, to listen again
to Archers episodes, including podcasts and an audio archive of the last
seven days. Official Fan Club: Archers Addicts www.archers-addicts.com

THE AUTHOR
Having spent his early career working as a farming journalist, Graham
Harvey joined the scriptwriting team of *The Archers* in 1984. Almost 600
episodes later he took over as Agricultural Story Editor, a sort of Farm
Minister for Ambridge. He considers it, quite simply, the best job in the
world.

WELCOME TO AMBRIDGE

After a momentous year in Ambridge we're back with the thirteenth edition of our handy guide to the characters and locations in *The Archers*.

This year has seen both triumphs and tragedies in the village beginning with the sad death of Nigel Pargetter and the subsequent rift between David Archer and his sister Elizabeth. Among the highlights of the year was the visit of the Duchess of Cornwall to Grey Gables. In between the tears and cheers life in Ambridge has continued in all its richness and delight.

This book will bring you fully up to date with all the stories that have entertained the listeners over the year. We hope you'll enjoy it.

Vanessa Whitburn
Editor, *The Archers*

FREQUENTLY ASKED QUESTIONS

When and how can I hear the programme?
On BBC Radio 4 (92–95 FM, 198 LW and on digital radio and television). Transmission times: 7pm Sunday to Friday, repeated at 2pm the next day, excluding Saturdays. An omnibus edition of the whole week's episodes is broadcast every Sunday at 10am. It can also be heard worldwide via podcasts or the BBC iPlayer (go to the Archers website: bbc.co.uk/archers).

How many people listen?
Nearly five million every week in the UK alone. *The Archers* is the most popular non-news programme on BBC Radio 4, and the most-listened-to BBC programme online.

How long has it been going?
Five pilot episodes were broadcast on the BBC Midlands Home Service in Whit Week 1950, but *The Archers*' first national broadcast was on 1 January 1951. Episode 16,300 went out on the 60th anniversary weekend, making this comfortably the world's longest-running drama series.

How did it start?

The creator of *The Archers*, Godfrey Baseley, devised the programme as a means of educating farmers in modern production methods when Britain was still subject to food rationing.

So it's an educational programme?

Not any more. *The Archers* lost its original educational remit in the early 1970s – but it still prides itself on the quality of its research and its reflection of real rural life.

How is it planned and written?

The Editor, Vanessa Whitburn, leads a ten-strong production team and nine writers as they plot the complicated lives of the families in Ambridge, looking ahead months or sometimes years in biannual long-term meetings. The detailed planning is done at monthly script meetings about two months ahead of transmission. Each writer produces a week's worth of scripts in a remarkable 13 days.

... and recorded?

Actors receive their scripts a few days before recording, which takes place every four weeks in a state-of-the-art studio at the BBC's premises in the Mailbox complex in central Birmingham. Twenty-four episodes are recorded digitally in six intensive days, using only two hours of studio time per thirteen-minute episode. This schedule means that being an *Archers* actor is by no means a full-time job, even for major characters, so many also have careers in film, theatre, television or other radio drama.

What's that 'dum-di-dum' tune?

The Archers' signature tune is a 'maypole dance': 'Barwick Green', from the suite *My Native Heath* by Yorkshire composer Arthur Wood.

How did you get that news item in?

Episodes are transmitted three to six weeks after recording. But listeners are occasionally intrigued to hear topical events reflected in that evening's broadcast, a feat achieved through a flurry of rewriting, re-recording and editing on the day of transmission.

CHARACTERS BY FORENAME

The characters in this book are listed alphabetically by surname or nickname. If you only know the forename, this should help you locate the relevant entry.

Abbie Tucker
Adam Macy
Alan Franks
Alice Carter
Alistair Lloyd
Amy Franks
Annabelle
   Schrivener
Ben Archer
Bert Fry
Brenda Tucker
Brian Aldridge
Caroline Sterling
Christine Barford
Christopher Carter
Clarrie Grundy
Clive Horrobin
Coriander Snell
Daniel Hebden
   Lloyd
David Archer
Debbie Aldridge
Ed Grundy
Eddie Grundy
Elizabeth Pargetter
Elona Makepeace
Emma Grundy
Fallon Rogers
Freda Fry
George Grundy
Graham Ryder
Harry Mason

Hayley Tucker
Hazel Woolley
Heather Pritchard
Helen Archer
Henry Archer
Ian Craig
Izzy Blake
Jack Woolley
Jake Hanson
James Bellamy
Jamie Perks
Jazzer McCreary
Jennifer Aldridge
Jill Archer
Jim Lloyd
Joe Grundy
Jolene Perks
Josh Archer
Kate Madikane
Kathy Perks
Kenton Archer
Kirsty Miller
Leonie Snell
Lewis Carmichael
Lilian Bellamy
Lily and Freddie
   Pargetter
Lorna Gibbs
Lucas Madikane
Lynda Snell
Mabel Thompson
Marty Bryant

Matt Crawford
Maurice Horton
Mike Tucker
Mia Hanson
Natalie Hollins
Neil Carter
Nic Hanson
Oliver Sterling
Pat Archer
Patrick Hennessey
Paul Morgan
Peggy Woolley
Phoebe Aldridge
Pip Archer
Rhys Williams
Robert Snell
Roy Tucker
Ruairi Donovan
Ruth Archer
Satya Khanna
Shiv Gupta
Shula Hebden
   Lloyd
Spencer Wilkes
Susan Carter
Ted Griffiths
Tom Archer
Tony Archer
Usha Franks
Vicky Tucker
William Grundy

Some can also be found under 'Silent Characters'

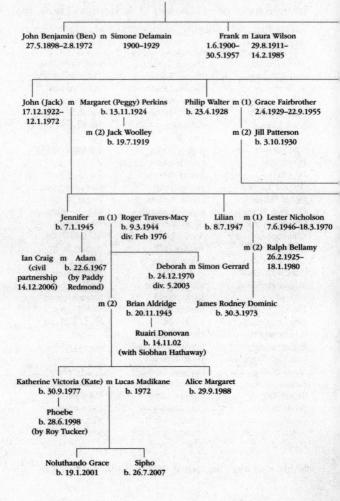

John Archer m Phoebe

John Benjamin (Ben) m Simone Delamain
27.5.1898–2.8.1972   1900–1929

Frank m Laura Wilson
1.6.1900–   29.8.1911–
30.5.1957   14.2.1985

John (Jack) m Margaret (Peggy) Perkins
17.12.1922–   b. 13.11.1924
12.1.1972

m (2) Jack Woolley
b. 19.7.1919

Philip Walter m (1) Grace Fairbrother
b. 23.4.1928   2.4.1929–22.9.1955

m (2) Jill Patterson
b. 3.10.1930

Jennifer   m (1) Roger Travers-Macy
b. 7.1.1945   b. 9.3.1944
                   div. Feb 1976

Lilian   m (1) Lester Nicholson
b. 8.7.1947   7.6.1946–18.3.1970

m (2) Ralph Bellamy
26.2.1925–
18.1.1980

Ian Craig   m   Adam
(civil   b. 22.6.1967
partnership   (by Paddy
14.12.2006)   Redmond)

Deborah m Simon Gerrard
b. 24.12.1970
div. 5.2003

James Rodney Dominic
b. 30.3.1973

m (2)   Brian Aldridge
b. 20.11.1943

Ruairi Donovan
b. 14.11.02
(with Siobhan Hathaway)

Katherine Victoria (Kate) m Lucas Madikane
b. 30.9.1977   b. 1972

Alice Margaret
b. 29.9.1988

Phoebe
b. 28.6.1998
(by Roy Tucker)

Noluthando Grace   Sipho
b. 19.1.2001   b. 26.7.2007

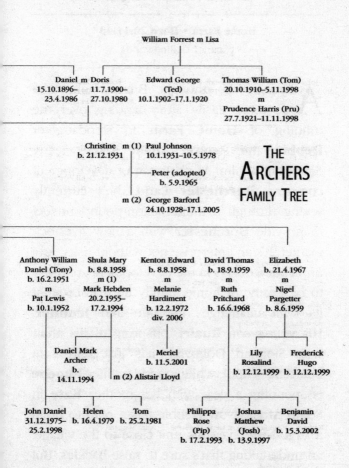

William Forrest m Lisa

Daniel m Doris
15.10.1896– 11.7.1900–
23.4.1986 27.10.1980

Edward George
(Ted)
10.1.1902–17.1.1920

Thomas William (Tom)
20.10.1910–5.11.1998
m
Prudence Harris (Pru)
27.7.1921–11.11.1998

Christine m (1) Paul Johnson
b. 21.12.1931   10.1.1931–10.5.1978

Peter (adopted)
b. 5.9.1965

m (2) George Barford
24.10.1928–17.1.2005

THE
ARCHERS
FAMILY TREE

Anthony William
Daniel (Tony)
b. 16.2.1951
m
Pat Lewis
b. 10.1.1952

Shula Mary
b. 8.8.1958
m (1)
Mark Hebden
20.2.1955–
17.2.1994

Kenton Edward
b. 8.8.1958
m
Melanie
Hardiment
b. 12.2.1972
div. 2006

David Thomas
b. 18.9.1959
m
Ruth
Pritchard
b. 16.6.1968

Elizabeth
b. 21.4.1967
m
Nigel
Pargetter
b. 8.6.1959

Daniel Mark
Archer
b.
14.11.1994

Meriel
b. 11.5.2001

m (2) Alistair Lloyd

Lily
Rosalind
b. 12.12.1999

Frederick
Hugo
b. 12.12.1999

John Daniel
31.12.1975–
25.2.1998

Helen
b. 16.4.1979

Tom
b. 25.2.1981

Philippa
Rose
(Pip)
b. 17.2.1993

Joshua
Matthew
(Josh)
b. 13.9.1997

Benjamin
David
b. 15.3.2002

BRIAN ALDRIDGE

Home Farm • Born 20.11.43

(Charles Collingwood)

Anyone who thought Brian might take life more easily after handing over the running of **Home Farm** to stepdaughter **Debbie** and stepson **Adam Macy** clearly didn't know him. As chairman of development company **Borchester Land**, he's currently seeing through a multi-million-pound project to provide **Borchester** with a new livestock market. It's an enterprise not without risks. Any unplanned delays in the development are likely to be costly. At home, family life has brought its own challenges for him and **Jennifer**. His young son **Ruairi**, offspring of his affair with Siobhan Donovan, has just started at boarding school, while granddaughter **Phoebe** is spending a year with her mother **Kate** in South Africa. Now Debbie has a plan to build a large-scale livestock unit close to the village, an undertaking that's sure to raise hackles. But few would bet on Brian, the ultimate smooth operator, not seeing it through.

DEBBIE ALDRIDGE

(née Travers-Macy, formerly Gerrard)
Home Farm • Born 24.12.70
(Tamsin Greig)

Debbie hasn't always had an easy relationship with her stepfather **Brian**, not least during his affair with Siobhan Donovan. This is one reason why she has been happy looking after Brian's farming interests in Hungary, making her just an occasional visitor to **Ambridge**. Even so, she has managed to exert her own influence on the running of **Home Farm**, sometimes annoying her half-brother and farming partner **Adam Macy** in the process. These days she's getting on a lot better with Brian. She shares his drive and restless ambition, and is clearly impressed with the way he has pressed ahead with the new livestock market. So much so that she's now keen to get his backing for a project of her own – a big new livestock unit on **Estate** land. If it comes off, she and her stepfather will make a formidable business team.

JENNIFER ALDRIDGE

(née Archer, formerly Travers-Macy)
Home Farm • Born 7.1.45
(Angela Piper)

These are unsettling times for the woman who has always viewed family as the very centre of her life. **Ruairi**, son of her husband **Brian** and the late Siobhan Donovan, is now adjusting to life at boarding school. Her granddaughter **Phoebe** – just 13 – has got her wish of spending a year with her mother in South Africa. Jennifer's younger daughter **Alice**, living in **Ambridge** with husband and farrier **Chris Carter**, doesn't want cash from the family to help develop the business. The young couple insist that they will make their own way. All of which has left Jennifer wondering what her role is to be from now on. Even sister **Lilian**, in need of support while her partner **Matt Crawford** served a prison sentence, is now busy running a property business with him. There's still one person in need of Jennifer's support – her mother **Peggy**, whose husband **Jack Woolley** is suffering from Alzheimer's.

PHOEBE ALDRIDGE

Willow Farm • Born 28.6.98

(Lucy Morris)

Since Phoebe was born in a tepee at Glastonbury Festival, it was a fair bet that sooner or later something of her mother **Kate Madikane**'s freedom-loving spirit would show up. Since Kate moved to South Africa, Phoebe has grown up with her dad **Roy Tucker** and his wife **Hayley**, with doting grandmother **Jennifer** on hand. But Kate's return to **Ambridge** to study international development at nearby **Felpersham** University unsettled Phoebe. She decided she wanted to leave the village and **Borchester** Green secondary school and spend a year in South Africa living with her other family. Her decision led to much concern from Roy and Hayley, who suspected the decision was mainly down to the influence of 'irresponsible' Kate.

AMBRIDGE

Though it might be called a 'typical village' in the heart of England, Ambridge has enjoyed a pretty remarkable year. First there was a royal visit, with the Duchess of Cornwall attending a charity event at **Grey Gables**, an occasion which made a lasting impact on many local residents, not least **Lynda Snell**. Then there was the last-minute decision of the producers of *Gardeners' Question Time* on BBC Radio 4 to record the programme in Ambridge Village Hall. Thankfully, the village has emerged from these momentous happenings pretty much unscathed. It's true **The Bull** is welcoming rather more outside diners than it used to, and the village **community shop** appears to be attracting a good bit more passing trade. Other than that life in Ambridge goes on much as it always did.

AMBRIDGE COMMUNITY SHOP

After a few initial teething troubles, the village shop has now become a flourishing community-run resource. Owned for many years by local businessman **Jack Woolley**, the community takeover was made possible when Jack's wife **Peggy** agreed to lease it to the village at a peppercorn rent. It's now run chiefly by local volunteers under the team leaders **Jill Archer**, **Christine Barford**, **Jim Lloyd**, Sabrina Thwaite, **Shula Hebden Lloyd**, **Oliver Sterling** and Neville Booth. The only 'professional' on the team is manager **Susan Carter**, who ran it in its former days. A good range of fresh, local produce sets this shop apart from many village stores. Above the shop is a small flat, reached by its own outside staircase. The present tenant is **Rhys Williams**, barman at **The Bull** public house.

AMBRIDGE GOLF CLUB

Originally part of **Grey Gables**, it was sold to land-and-property company **Borchester Land** in 2006, along with the country park. So it's now part of **Brian Aldridge**'s sizeable empire. Under director of golf Leigh Barham, the club has grown in popularity in recent years, though it has taken something of a hit during the recession. Clubhouse catering manager **Kathy Perks**, who took over in 2008, has extended the restaurant menu, making it a popular lunch venue. It's a facility greatly enjoyed by **Lilian Bellamy**, who's now sometimes seen there with her partner – in life and in business – **Matt Crawford**. Matt enjoys a round on the nine-hole course and finds it a good place to do business.

AMBRIDGE HALL

Following a chance encounter with the Duchess of Cornwall during a royal visit to **Grey Gables**, **Lynda Snell** – mein host at one of the county's top B&Bs – wasted no time in updating the Ambridge Hall website and publicity material. All now mention the royal visit and Lynda's part in it. There are plenty of visitors who return time and time again thanks to the relaxed atmosphere created by Lynda and her husband **Robert**. Inside, the tasteful décor is guided by Lynda's powers of feng shui. Outside, a Welsh slate patio (designed by the owner and built by local craftsmen) and mature garden with a 'low-allergen' area, are sources of much spiritual refreshment. The quiet gardens run down to the River Am, where a local naturalist has confirmed the occasional appearance of kingfishers and otters. More active visitors sometimes venture into the paddock to meet the hall's resident llamas – Constanza, Wolfgang and Salieri.

AMBRIDGE ORGANICS

Harcourt Road, Borchester

Though managed by **Helen Archer**, daughter of local farmers **Pat** and **Tony**, who own the shop, the day-to-day running is mostly in the hands of **Kirsty Miller**. With its aim of bringing the 'farm shop experience to the centre of town', Ambridge Organics was very much the creation of Helen, whose own cheese is sold in the shop. These days, Helen is too preoccupied with her young son **Henry** to devote the time she once gave to the business. However, the capable and resourceful Kirsty is ably assisted by Anja from Poland. Helen continues to take a real though less hands-on interest in the business. Like other organic businesses, Ambridge Organics seems to have weathered the initial effects of the recession and is seeing something of a resurgence in demand for its locally sourced vegetables, salads, meats and dairy products, plus ethically sourced speciality foods. Sadly a severe setback at the parent business – **Bridge Farm** – has taken the shine off recent gains.

BEN ARCHER

Brookfield Farm • Born 15.3.02

(Thomas Lester)

The younger brother of **Pip** and **Josh Archer**, Ben is the only one of **Ruth** and **David**'s brood so far to have shown little interest in the farm. His life is mostly dominated by computer gaming, sport and squabbling with his older brother. But recently he has been seen playing a computer game on farming. David's hoping this may mark the awakening of an interest in the family business and that before long he'll be offering to help milk the cows along with his brother Josh.

DAVID ARCHER

Brookfield Farm • Born 18.9.59

(Timothy Bentinck)

David's life has been overshadowed by the tragic events at **Lower Loxley** early in the New Year. Following a family party, David and his brother-in-law Nigel Pargetter ventured onto the roof on a frosty evening to remove a banner. Nigel slipped and fell to his death. Horrified by his part in the tragedy, David devoted himself to supporting his sister as she bravely battled to hold her life and business together for the sake of her twins, **Lily** and **Freddie**. But when **Elizabeth** discovered that David played a key role in the decision to go up on the roof that night, she turned on him, blaming him for Nigel's death. David was devastated. He tried to lose himself in running the farm and in his duties as chair of the local National Farmers' Union branch. But only the unswerving support of his wife **Ruth** has enabled him to keep going. Meanwhile David's sister **Shula** does her best to heal the rift with Elizabeth.

HELEN ARCHER

Bridge Farm • Born 16.4.79

(Louiza Patikas)

For **Pat** and **Tony Archer**'s daughter, life was transformed by a single event at the very start of the year – the birth of her son, **Henry**. Over the years, life has been tough for Helen. The loss of her partner Greg Turner led to anorexia, followed by a period of destructive drinking and partying. The arrival of Greg's young daughter, Annette Turner, seemed to add a new purpose to life, but when the girl left abruptly Helen was once more left alone. In the face of disapproval from her father Tony, she decided to have a child of her own by sperm donation. The arrival of Henry brought her real happiness, perhaps for the first time in her life. Family and friends have observed a new serenity about her. Even the way she runs her business – **Ambridge Organics** – seems calmer and less frantic. Perhaps best of all, her father Tony is delighted with his new grandson.

HENRY ARCHER

Bridge Farm • Born 2.1.11

Helen's son – conceived by sperm donation – was delivered by emergency Caesarean section when she developed eclampsia during pregnancy. Though Helen's father **Tony Archer** had found it hard to accept Helen's decision to have a child this way, the possibility that he might lose them both came as a severe shock to him. He is now devoted to the boy. It's clear to most people in the village that Henry has brought a new serenity to his mother's life. Sadly for some in the community his birth will always be associated with the tragic night that Nigel Pargetter met his death.

JILL ARCHER

(née Patterson)

Glebe Cottage • Born 3.10.30

(Patricia Greene)

Like all the Archer family, Jill has been shocked by the tragic death of her son-in-law Nigel Pargetter and the subsequent bitter rift between her daughter **Elizabeth** and her son **David**, whom Elizabeth blames for the death. To Jill, for whom family means everything, these events would always have been hard to bear. But coming so soon after the death of her own beloved husband Phil in 2010, they seemed particularly cruel. As always Jill's first instinct was to try to heal the hurts that have so deeply damaged the family. Her other offspring – son **Kenton** and daughter **Shula** – have rallied round in a bid to heal the wounds. But, however long it takes, no one doubts Jill's strength and staying power. As long as there's breath in her body, she'll go on being there for the family whenever they need her.

JOSH ARCHER

Brookfield Farm • Born 13.9.97

(Cian Cheesbrough)

Farmers **David** and **Ruth Archer** have always encouraged their children to be entrepreneurial. But they can't help wondering if their middle child Josh hasn't taken it rather too much to heart. When he learned there were crayfish in the River Am, the resourceful teenager reckoned he knew a good business opportunity when he saw one. He approached his Uncle **Kenton**, partner of village pub landlady **Jolene Perks**, and soon locally sourced crayfish were on the menu of **The Bull**. When local gamekeeper **Will Grundy** discovered young Josh catching crayfish, he took steps to put a stop to the enterprise. When Ruth got to hear about it, she wasn't best pleased with her brother-in-law Kenton for encouraging the boy. But on the quiet she and David can't help admiring their son's business acumen.

KENTON ARCHER

April Cottage • Born 8.8.58

(Richard Attlee)

Kenton is rapidly making himself something of a force in the world of catering. Having transformed the homely **Jaxx** café-bar in **Borchester** into the place to be for the county's young professionals, he's now busy improving the food on offer at his new home, **The Bull**. Locally sourced foods such as venison and Hereford beef are now more regularly on the menu. Mind you, Kenton's decision to move in with pub landlady **Jolene Perks** didn't go down well with everyone, not least his ex-partner **Kathy**. But Kathy would have to admit that he has been a steadying influence on her wayward teenage son **Jamie**. Kenton has also become a significant figure in the lives of his young nephew and niece, twins **Freddie** and **Lily Pargetter**, who lost their father Nigel so tragically.

PAT ARCHER

(née Lewis)
Bridge Farm • Born 10.1.52
(Patricia Gallimore)

No one believes in good food more passionately than Pat. It's why she and husband **Tony** converted **Bridge Farm** to organic and started marketing their own dairy products many years ago. So it seems particularly cruel that it's their business that has been hit by a local outbreak of E. coli infection. The outbreak was traced back to Pat's ice cream and, though the public health authorities decided to take no further action against the business, sales of Bridge Farm organic dairy foods, built up so painstakingly over many years, have plummeted. With losses mounting, Pat views with mounting despair the collapse of her life's work. Her hope for the future is in the resilience and resourcefulness of son **Tom** and daughter **Helen**. For consolation, there's always her beautiful new grandson **Henry**.

PIP ARCHER

Brookfield Farm • Born 17.2.93

(Helen Monks)

Farming is in the blood of **David** and **Ruth Archer**'s eldest child, and now she's in a settled relationship with **Spencer** – son of a local arable farmer – there's no holding her back. Even before she began her degree course at **Felpersham** University – in Agriculture and Farming Business Management – she came up with ambitious plans to improve the marketing of the **Brookfield Farm** lambs. She remains a keen member of the local Young Farmers branch. She's also interested in the wildlife at Brookfield Farm, particularly the barn owls. After the traumas of her ill-fated relationship with Jude Simpson – a college student twelve years her senior – she seems to be back in control of her life, much to the relief of her parents.

RUTH ARCHER

(née Pritchard)
Brookfield Farm • Born 16.6.68
(Felicity Finch)

The tragic rift between Ruth's husband **David** and his sister **Elizabeth** following the accidental death of Elizabeth's husband Nigel has cast a long shadow over **Brookfield Farm**. With David haunted by guilt over the event, Ruth is determined to hold the family – and the farm – together. Having played a key role in making the dairy herd an efficient, grass-based operation, she has now resolved to ensure its continued success for the sake of their children, **Pip**, **Josh** and **Ben**. For this Northumberland girl, dealing with difficulties has almost become second nature. She has already had to deal with breast cancer and a brief affair that threatened to break up all she and David had achieved. She's not about to let the events at **Lower Loxley** – however terrible – spoil things now.

TOM ARCHER

1, The Green • Born 25.2.81

(Tom Graham)

With his established meat products business, Tom was anxious to marry and start a family with fiancée **Brenda Tucker**. But Brenda made it clear she was in no great hurry to take this next big step in their relationship. She's rather enjoyed the excitement of working for local property developers **Matt Crawford** and **Lilian Bellamy**. All thoughts of marriage have now been dismissed – even by Tom – following a crisis at the family farm. A local outbreak of E. coli infection was traced back to **Bridge Farm** dairy and a lapse in hygiene standards by one of its employees. The resulting publicity and collapse in sales has put a huge financial strain on all the Bridge Farm operations, including Tom's enterprises. He now realises that the urgent priority is not to start a family but to save the family farm.

TONY ARCHER

Bridge Farm • Born 16.2.51

(Colin Skipp)

Now 60, Tony hoped that his life might be getting rather easier by now. Though he and his wife **Pat** took on a sizeable mortgage in order to buy the tenancy of **Bridge Farm**, having their offspring **Tom** and **Helen** working together on a fully integrated business was supposed to make for a smoother operation. Tony was also getting a lot of pleasure from his new grandson **Henry**, though he was initially very critical of Helen's decision to have a baby by sperm donation. But if Tony had hoped for an easier time, his hopes have been dashed. The tracing of an E. coli outbreak to dairy products supplied by Bridge Farm has put the whole operation under threat. It's another hard lesson that life seldom turns out the way you'd like it to be.

CHRISTINE BARFORD

(née Archer, formerly Johnson)
Woodbine Cottage • Born 21.12.31
(Lesley Saweard)

For Phil Archer's younger sister, the highlight of the year has been the visit of the *Gardeners' Question Time* team to **Ambridge**. Since she sold her riding stables to niece **Shula Hebden Lloyd**, retirement has been a quiet but happy time. She often visits London to see Peter, her adopted son by her first marriage. He phones regularly and always remembers her birthday. She is also in regular contact with Terry, the son of her second husband George Barford. Apart from her duties as churchwarden she is content to play a mainly supporting role in village events. Having witnessed the tragic death of George following the fire-bombing of their house – a crime that earned arsonist **Clive Horrobin** a 12-year sentence – Chris is happy with the quiet life. However, the visit of GQT was a welcome exception. She has also formed a charming friendship with **Jim Lloyd**, with whom she shares an interest in gardening.

JAMES BELLAMY

Born 30.3.73

(Roger May)

James's infrequent visits to his mother **Lilian** were chiefly motivated by concern over his inheritance. Lilian's growing business involvement with her partner – property developer and ex-jailbird **Matt Crawford** – has added to his anxieties. Recently, however, James has had another reason for visiting **Ambridge** – his new relationship with **Leonie Snell**, daughter of **Robert Snell**, who lives at **Ambridge Hall** with his second wife **Lynda**. The relationship came as a surprise to both Lilian and Robert. So did the fact that the couple were writing a book on country life together focusing on Ambridge.

LILIAN BELLAMY

(née Archer, formerly Nicholson)
The Dower House • Born 8.7.47
(Sunny Ormonde)

No one would dispute that **Jennifer**'s sister has been the making of property developer and general wheeler-dealer **Matt Crawford**. Matt's colourful career reached a low point when he was imprisoned for fraud. But, despite a fleeting romantic attachment to his half-brother, builder **Paul Morgan**, Lilian remained true to her man. Following his release, she helped him get back on his feet by setting up a property business in which they now both work. As with their personal relationship, the business relationship between the fiery pair is not without its squalls. Lilian is not totally convinced that Matt is honouring his undertaking to be open about his business dealings. And Matt was not best pleased when she offered to let one of their rental properties to care home assistant **Elona Makepeace**, after pressure from Lilian's mother, **Peggy Woolley**. However, for all their many battles, the couple look very solid.

IZZY BLAKE

Meadow Rise, Borchester • Born 1993

(Lizzie Wofford)

How well Izzy's relationship with **Pip Archer**, her best friend from **Borchester** Green school, will weather Pip's move to **Felpersham** University is anyone's guess. Izzy has never had much interest in academic work. Rather than stay on at college for her A levels as Pip did, she chose instead a job on a supermarket checkout. Even so, the two young women appear to have a strong relationship. Somehow it weathered Pip's stormy affair with the much older Jude Simpson, though it was Izzy who revealed his true age to Pip's worried parents. In calmer times, it's a fair bet the friendship will endure.

BORCHESTER

Sadly **Borsetshire**'s principal market town has not escaped the recession. Over the past twelve months, a number of town centre shops have become vacant, while others have become charity shops. Several of the up-market apartments in the smart development alongside the Old Wool Market now display 'For Sale' or 'To Let' signs. The footfall in **Underwoods**, the town's own department store, has dropped substantially since Christmas. Even the refurbished **Jaxx** café-bar in Oriel Road, though popular, has its quiet days, while **Ambridge Organics** in Harcourt Road has noticeably more special offers these days. Local business people are hoping the new retail development planned for the present livestock market site will kick-start the recovery when it comes on stream next year.

BORCHESTER LAND

Under chairman **Brian Aldridge**, this go-ahead land development company clearly has its sights set on big things. The company is currently developing a new livestock market on a greenfield site on the town bypass. The aim is to free up the present town centre site for redevelopment as a retail and commercial centre. It's a bold step for this regional company, particularly as they've agreed to a tight completion date. The gossip is that its former chairman, the disgraced **Matt Crawford**, who spent several months in prison for fraud, is continuing to influence company policy through his partner **Lilian Bellamy**, who sits on the board of the off-shoot company set up to run the market. Following past boardroom tussles there's little love lost between Crawford and Aldridge. Whoever's pulling the strings, it's clear the company has big ambitions. The company's assets in **Ambridge** include the pheasant shoot, run by head keeper **Will Grundy**, and the business units at Sawyer's Farm.

BORSETSHIRE

Despite the downturn in the economy, this unprepossessing county of farmland and quiet rivers continues to punch above its weight as far as tourist numbers are concerned. Walkers are drawn to the fine range of hills – the Hassetts – while culture hunters gravitate towards the charming cathedral city of **Felpersham**, with its art gallery and museum. The county's two main newspapers – the *Felpersham Advertiser* and the ***Borchester*** *Echo* – somehow manage to keep going despite the collapse in the small-ad market. Rigorous cost-cutting has meant a number of journalists have been made redundant. Against the trend, the county magazine *Borsetshire Life* remains popular and profitable. One of the communities featured in the past year has been the picturesque village of **Ambridge** in the south of the county, a few miles from the Hassett Hills.

BRIDGE FARM

LAND
140 acres owned plus 32 acres rented

STOCK
92 milking cows (Friesians) • 45 followers (heifers/calves) 45 fattening pigs

CROPS
113 acres grassland • 10 acres barley • 27 acres wheat • 5 acres potatoes • 4 acres carrots • 2 acres leeks • 3 acres swedes • 2 acres Dutch cabbage • 1 acre Savoy cabbage • 5 acres mixed vegetable and salad crops, including two poly-tunnels

LABOUR
Tony Archer • **Pat Archer** • **Tom Archer** • **Helen Archer** **Jazzer McCreary** (part-time, pigs) • **Susan Carter** (part-time, dairy)

Tony and Pat Archer's long-established organic farm has taken a severe knock following an outbreak of E. coli infection which was traced back to the farm dairy. The attendant publicity has severely damaged the farm's hard-won markets for dairy produce and processed meat products. The economic fallout has been especially severe as the business currently carries a sizeable mortgage following a buy-out of the tenancy from **Borchester Land**. On the plus side, this is a family business with a new generation of the Archer family, Helen and Tom, running their own enterprises. Family and friends are hopeful that with the support of their loyal staff they'll turn the business round.

BROOKFIELD FARM

LAND
469 acres owned

STOCK
176 milking cows (Friesians) • 76 followers (heifers – some
Brown Swiss crosses) • 82 beef cattle (Herefords) • 350 ewes
a few hens

CROPS
344 acres grassland • 85 acres cereals • 10 acres oilseed rape
8 acres potatoes • 12 acres beans • 10 acres forage maize

LABOUR
David Archer (managing) • **Ruth Archer** (dairy herd manager)
Eddie Grundy (relief herdsperson) • **Bert Fry** (retired, casual)
Biff, Tig (sheepdogs)

Brookfield is a medium-sized family farm in south **Borsetshire**. It's unusual in having a wider range of enterprises than most farms in the area which have become more specialist units. David and Ruth Archer have stuck with a mixed farming system, believing it to be both productive biologically and resilient financially. They operate a rotational grass paddock system for the dairy cows and raise high-quality, grass-fed beef for sale direct. Arable is managed on contract by nearby **Home Farm**. **Pip Archer**, one of the new generation at Brookfield, is currently studying at **Felpersham** University.

MARTY BRYANT

Lakey Green
(Ralph Davis)

A chum of **Jamie Perks**, Marty is too easily influenced for his own good, especially by the likes of Steve Wilkes, the tearaway brother of **Pip Archer**'s boyfriend **Spencer**. When Steve stole a car and demanded that his two mates jump in, it was Marty who did as he was told – if reluctantly – and Jamie who refused. When Steve subsequently crashed the car, Marty found himself in court too. Like Steve, he was given a nine-month Referral Order plus a driving ban. If he wants a good future, Marty would be well advised to keep Jamie as a mate but drop the dangerous Steve.

THE BULL

Since **Kenton Archer** teamed up with landlady **Jolene Perks**, this once popular south **Borsetshire** hostelry has seen something of a revival in its fortunes. Following the death of former landlord – the popular Sid Perks – in New Zealand, the pub went into a fallow period. Trade dipped sharply and for a brief time there was a real possibility of it closing. Under the new management team, however, trade has picked up substantially. In the restaurant, the menu has been refreshed and now features a number of foods from local suppliers. These include venison from **Home Farm** and grass-fed Hereford beef from **Brookfield Farm**. The improved catering is the idea of Kenton who also runs **Jaxx** café-bar in **Borchester**.

LEWIS CARMICHAEL

Lower Loxley Hall
(Robert Lister)

Following the death of his wife Julia Pargetter, Lewis has mostly been engaged in helping out in the **Lower Loxley** art gallery and occasionally sampling the Lower Loxley wines. An old friend of the Pargetters, he expected to settle into a quiet retirement of reading and compiling his history of the Pargetter family. But, following the tragic and untimely death of Nigel, he found himself playing a much bigger role in the running of the house. In fact, in the weeks immediately after the accident his unstinting support of **Elizabeth** and the children helped the family get through this difficult period. With **Roy Tucker** in place as manager, Lewis is now able to take life a little easier. But Elizabeth's observation that 'Every fine old house needs a Lewis around to worry about it' is perhaps truer than she could have imagined.

ALICE CARTER

Home Farm Cottage • Born 29.9.88

(Hollie Chapman)

Alice's surprise marriage to hunky young farrier **Christopher Carter** shocked her mother **Jennifer** and amused pretty well everyone else in the village. However, the modern marriage of this attractive young couple seems so full of happiness that even Jennifer has begun to see it as a success. After three years at Southampton University – which was not without its difficulties – Alice is now back in **Ambridge**, and the young couple are together full-time. Ambitious Christopher has invested in a new van and mobile forge, and the couple are saving up to buy the farrier business of Chris's boss, Ronnie, when he retires next year.

CHRISTOPHER CARTER

Home Farm Cottage • Born 22.6.88

(William Sanderson-Thwaite)

The son of **Neil** and **Susan Carter** seems one of those lucky people on whom the sun always shines. In this case, it has bronzed his well-developed biceps and ensured that his farrier services are in constant demand from some of the county's poshest horse-owning families. He even won the village Single Wicket Competition in cricket. It's hard to see how he can fail to end up with a very substantial business, particularly now he has the support of his wife, the lovely **Alice**, daughter of **Jennifer** and **Brian Aldridge**. The couple recently suffered a setback, though, when they took out a seemingly cheap loan for a new van and mobile forge. The 'loan shark' in Southampton – where Alice was at university – had taken a shine to her, and the loan came with strings attached. Buying themselves out of the deal meant taking out a far more costly loan, putting the couple under financial pressure. Even so, no one would bet against the ambitious Chris making a success of the business.

NEIL CARTER

Ambridge View • Born 22.5.57
(Brian Hewlett)

Pig farmer Neil is one of those people who seem made for hard work. Nothing has come easily to him since the days he managed Phil Archer's pig unit at Hollowtree Farm. These days he has his own small herd of Gloucester Old Spots, selling the organic weaners to fatteners like **Tom Archer** at **Bridge Farm**. With **Hayley Tucker** he also runs a small flock of organic, free-range hens. For a man in his mid fifties it's a tough life, particularly on a frosty winter morning when the drinkers have frozen up and the pigs have to be watered by bowser. But it would be wrong to think of Neil as one dimensional. He's a bell-ringer – tower captain at **St Stephen's** – a keen cricketer, churchwarden and chair of the Parish Council. Best of all he's a grandfather again. Daughter **Emma**, partner of dairy farmer **Ed Grundy**, has a new baby girl, **Keira Susan**, half-sister to **George**.

SUSAN CARTER

(née Horrobin)
Ambridge View • Born 10.10.63
(Charlotte Martin)

Being married to a small-scale pig farmer, Susan is used to financial insecurity. It's what makes her own jobs – postmistress and chief stock controller at **Ambridge Community Shop**, and part-time dairy assistant at **Bridge Farm** – vital to the family income. So the crisis at Bridge Farm, threatened with financial meltdown following an outbreak of E. coli infection, has come as a real worry. The bright spot in Susan's life is her new granddaughter **Keira Susan**, born to daughter **Emma** and her partner, dairy farmer **Ed Grundy**. Secretly, she's hoping for a similar happy event for **Alice**, her daughter-in-law, from the landed **Aldridge** family. For the socially aspiring Susan, this would be proof that her branch of the **Horrobin** family had escaped their lowly roots.

CASA NUEVA

The remote hideaway home of gamekeeper **Will Grundy** and his partner **Nic Hanson** along with her two children, **Jake** and **Mia**. The tied cottage is owned by Will's bosses, **Borchester Land**, owners of the **Estate**. Will once lived there with his first love **Emma Grundy** following the couple's return from their Mexican honeymoon, but the ill-fated marriage wasn't to last and Emma went off with Will's younger brother **Ed**. These days Will has found happiness at Casa Nueva with his new family. It's remote but handy for Will's shoot. Townie Nic is starting to get used to it now she has learnt to drive.

IAN CRAIG

Honeysuckle Cottage • Born 1970

(Stephen Kennedy)

Unlike the stereotype, the popular head chef at **Grey Gables** has seldom thrown a tantrum in the kitchen. It's perhaps because he's basically happy and settled in this small rural community where he's the civil partner of farmer **Adam Macy**. He once harboured thoughts of parenthood, particularly when the chance arose to father a child with his long-time friend Mads. Her change of mind caused him much sadness, though in retrospect he admits it probably saved his relationship with Adam. His deepening friendship with **Helen Archer** – and her baby son **Henry**, conceived by sperm donation – has helped him get over his personal disappointment. The year has held another highlight: the Duchess of Cornwall complimented him on his shortcake biscuits.

MATT CRAWFORD

The Dower House • Born 7.8.47

(Kim Durham)

A brief term of imprisonment for fraud seems to have done nothing to lessen Matt's desire for success. Unfortunately, his prison record means he can't play his business power games directly any more. So he's found a way of pursuing his ambitions through a surrogate – his partner **Lilian Bellamy**. Through his impressive contacts on the **Borsetshire** development scene, he managed to block his former company **Borchester Land**'s big livestock market development. His price for allowing the project to go ahead? A seat on the board of the new company for Lilian. When she went into business with Matt, Lilian made it clear she'd be no stooge. But behind some of the power games she plays, fellow board member **Brian Aldridge** senses the unseen hand of would-be mogul Matt.

RUAIRI DONOVAN

Home Farm • Born 14.11.02

(Ciaran Coyle)

Ruairi, the love-child of **Brian Aldridge** and the late Siobhan Hathaway, is now a much-loved member of the Aldridge family. **Jennifer**, whose long marriage to Brian looked like ending when news of the affair came out, found herself shedding a tear when the boy went off to boarding school. The other Aldridge offspring – **Debbie**, **Adam**, **Kate** and **Alice** have all taken Ruairi to their hearts. The boy, whose appearance once looked like tearing a family apart, now seems to have made it stronger than ever.

THE ESTATE

Originally called the Berrow Estate, the 1,020-acre arable block is now part of the land and property portfolio of **Borchester Land**. It is farmed on contract by **Home Farm**, with day-to-day management being carried out by **Adam Macy**. Principally an arable operation, it has been farmed for high yields using the full range of inputs. **Debbie Aldridge**, in overall charge from her base in Hungary, has proposed a big-scale intensive dairy enterprise to add value to the Estate's cereal crop. Whatever the outcome, the controversial plan looks sure to upset the village.

FELPERSHAM

Unlike the market town of **Borchester**, the cathedral city seems to have weathered the recession pretty well so far. This is in part due to the impressive range of up-market shops catering for a group whose wealth seems unaffected by the downturn in the economy. Even so, those who know the city well have noticed that in certain areas it has started looking a touch down at heel. Despite this, gourmet eating places such as the Quince Tree seem as popular as ever, and the gaggle of gastro pubs and bistros by the river are invariably packed on Friday and Saturday nights. The clutch of high-tech companies that have relocated to Felpersham from Birmingham and London in recent years are generally doing pretty well, though there have been a few redundancies. The local chamber of commerce is confident that Felpersham will be among the leaders of the recovery.

ALAN FRANKS

The Vicarage, Ambridge
(John Telfer)

It's tempting to think of the rural vicar's life as an endless round of fêtes, jumble sales and Sunday worship. Certainly there's no shortage of these in the parish life of **Ambridge**'s motorcycling vicar. But in any small community there are sometimes momentous events that shake the comfortable order of things and propel the spiritual leader into a tangle of grief, recrimination and pain. One such event was the tragic death in an accident of local landowner Nigel Pargetter. Quite apart from the sorrow and loss caused, the event has split apart one of Ambridge's central families – the **Archers**. Alan has needed all his pastoral skills to try and bring some healing and reconciliation to the situation. It's at times like this that Alan truly knows what he's there for. And he's never more thankful to have the support of his Hindu wife **Usha**.

AMY FRANKS

The Vicarage, Ambridge • Born 1989

(Vinette Robinson)

Once the best friend of **Alice Carter**, the Reverend **Alan**'s mixed-race daughter by his first wife Catherine, now works as a midwife at **Felpersham** Hospital. It was her keen-eyed observation of **Helen Archer** at a family party that led to the early diagnosis of eclampsia, which may have saved the life of baby **Henry**. Amy is quick to support her father whenever she feels he's right, though she is too much her own woman to side with him without thinking through the issue. Over his relationship with **Usha** – one which caused considerable controversy in the village – she has been unswerving in her support.

USHA FRANKS

(née Gupta)
The Vicarage, Ambridge • Born 17.6.62
(Souad Faress)

It was Hindu Usha's marriage to Church of England vicar **Alan Franks** that led to the resignation of long-standing churchwarden **Shula Hebden Lloyd**. Much of the fuss caused by the marriage has now subsided and her appearance with Alan at church and social events is now generally accepted in the parish. Not that Usha is in any sense a stereotypical 'vicar's wife'. A qualified solicitor, she is a partner in local law firm Jefferson Crabtree. She's also a keen runner and, when time permits, a member of the **Ambridge** Bookclub, which she helped to found.

BERT FRY

Brookfield Bungalow • Born 1936

(Eric Allan)

Though retired, former farm worker Bert remains a valuable asset at **Brookfield Farm**. With a range of farming skills, he can usually be relied upon to help out at busy times such as lambing or when there are lambs to sort out for market. He's also pretty hot at competitive ploughing. He's a stalwart in many of the local ploughing matches, entering the class for vintage tractors using the ageing Massey Ferguson bought for the purpose by **David Archer**. He's also a keen cricket umpire turning out regularly for **Ambridge** cricket team. And his entries for the village Flower and Produce Show are legendary. Bert's post-retirement activities extend as far as stately home tour guide. He's on the list of official guides at **Lower Loxley**, now run by **Elizabeth Pargetter** and her new manager **Roy Tucker**.

FREDA FRY

Brookfield Bungalow

Bert's wife of more than fifty years, Freda has been the unsung hero behind the food on offer at **The Bull**. Over the years, her home-made pies and casseroles have gained a considerable reputation. Following the death of pub landlord Sid Perks, the pub became a less happy place to work, and Freda more than once considered retirement. But since **Kenton Archer** started helping Sid's widow **Jolene**, the pub has become an altogether happier place. That said, Kenton, who also runs **Jaxx** café-bar in **Borchester**, has his own distinctive ideas about the menu. Just lately he has tried introducing new dishes onto Freda's specials board. For the traditionalist Freda, these aren't always a step in the right direction. When she's not working in The Bull, Freda is happy devoting herself to jam and pickle-making for the annual Flower and Produce Show.

LORNA GIBBS

(Alison Belbin)

The catering manager at **Lower Loxley Hall**, Lorna runs the café and shop. Following the arrival of **Roy Tucker** as general manager, both are being reorganised. However, it's likely that Lorna will emerge with extra responsibilities. Outside work, she helps occasionally with village events, and once did the make-up for the village Christmas panto. She is known for her good sense of humour

GRANGE FARM

STOCK
47 milkers (Guernseys)

CROPS
50 acres of grassland
(A further 50 acres of grass are rented from the Estate)

LABOUR
Ed Grundy (tenant farmer)
Mike Tucker (milk roundsman and dairy processor)
Harry Mason (milk roundsman)
Jazzer McCreary (milk roundsman – part-time)

The farming press may be full of stories about new mega-dairies, but the small herd at Grange Farm is still making a reasonable living for tenant farmer Ed Grundy and his family. The secret lies in processing the milk on-farm and selling direct to homes in **Ambridge** and neighbouring villages. The herd was established in 2006 by the farm owner **Oliver Sterling**, who was keen that self-employed milkman Mike Tucker should have a local product to sell. Oliver employed young Ed initially as herdsman. Following Oliver's retirement from active farming, he helped set up Ed in a Farm Business Tenancy, with low-interest loans to help him get started. Ed has now expanded the herd and rents extra acres from **Borchester Land**, owners of the **Estate**.

GRANGE SPINNEY

A newish mixed development of executive houses and 'affordable' homes, Grange Spinney is a monument to local developers **Borchester Land**. This was the company's first development in **Ambridge**, at a time when it was led by the now disgraced **Matt Crawford**. Chiefly a 'dormitory' development for commuters travelling in to **Borchester**, **Felpersham** and even Birmingham, it does have a few residents who are active in village life. Prominent among them are the Thwaites, Richard and Sabrina. Richard is on the Parish Council and is a keen member of the Ambridge Bookclub, while Sabrina is a volunteer helper in the village shop.

GREY GABLES

Set in idyllic grounds, this up-market country hotel has had an eventful year. The most notable event was a visit from the Duchess of Cornwall at a charity gathering. The visit marks the growing reputation of Grey Gables as one of the county's top hotels. It's particularly noted for its fine restaurant. Under head chef **Ian Craig**, it specialises in local dishes prepared where possible from local produce. But like most hotels it isn't immune from the effects of the economic downturn. Following the departure of deputy manager **Roy Tucker** for a top management post at nearby stately home **Lower Loxley**, hotel owner **Caroline Sterling** decided not to reappoint but to take on more of the day-to-day management herself. Grey Gables is becoming an increasingly popular choice for weddings.

TED GRIFFITHS

(Paul Webster)

Ted has become a good friend of **Peggy Woolley** as a result of her frequent visits to see her husband **Jack** in the Laurels nursing home. Ted visits the home to see his wife Violet who, like Jack, suffers from dementia. Ted, who was an art teacher in a local college before his retirement, has intrigued Peggy with his skill at enamelling, showing her a beautiful little box he's made. After a visit to his home workshop, Peggy expressed an interest in learning the art of enamelling herself. In a few workshop sessions, Ted taught Peggy and her sister-in-law **Jill Archer** the rudiments of the craft. Peggy made a tie-pin for Jack. Both Peggy and Jill decided to enter examples of their enamelling work in the village Flower and Produce Show.

CLARRIE GRUNDY

Keeper's Cottage • Born 12.5.54

(Rosalind Adams)

As if life wasn't tough enough for Clarrie, looking after husband **Eddie** and his ageing father **Joe**, she has been drawn into the on-going feud between her sons **Will** and **Ed**. When Ed's wife **Emma** gave birth to little **Keira Susan** it was a wonderful moment for Clarrie – a second grandchild to grow up with young **George**. However, Emma wasted no time in showing off her new baby to former husband Will, already annoyed that his son George was being brought up by Ed. Will's response was to put pressure on his partner **Nic Hanson** to have a baby with him, a half-brother or sister for her own two, **Jake** and **Mia**. But Nic was in no hurry to add to her family. Clarrie found herself drawn into this complicated family tussle. But soon Clarrie had problems of her own to worry about. As a result of her failure to follow food hygiene rules, the **Bridge Farm** dairy came under threat. An outbreak of E. coli infection contracted from Bridge Farm ice cream put the whole business at risk.

ED GRUNDY

Rickyard Cottage, Brookfield • Born 28.9.84

(Barry Farrimond)

Life's pretty good for **Eddie** and **Clarrie**'s younger son. The former wild boy who served community punishments for joy-riding and burglary is now a farmer with a fixed-term farm business tenancy at **Grange Farm**, owned by **Oliver Sterling**. He has his own herd of Guernsey cows and makes a reasonable living from them thanks to the higher price paid by local dairy-man **Mike Tucker**, who sells the milk direct to local homes. Farmer Ed is also living with his great love, **Emma**, who was formerly married to his brother **Will**. They are bringing up **George** – Emma's son by Will – and now have a child of their own, **Keira Susan Grundy**. All in all it's turned out pretty well for the former tearaway. His brother still thinks he's a waste of space, but that doesn't bother the happy Ed one iota.

EDDIE GRUNDY

Keeper's Cottage • Born 15.3.51

(Trevor Harrison)

In an ideal world, Eddie would have chosen to be the lifelong tenant of **Grange Farm**. But with farming economics firmly set against small tenant farmers – and Eddie's admittedly less than top-rate management skills – bankruptcy ended the dream. Through a mixture of hard work and his not inconsiderable entrepreneurial skills, Eddie has managed to carve himself out a decent living in the countryside. Mind you, to achieve it he's had to turn his hand to many things – market trading, relief milking, landscape gardening and patio construction, plus part-time work at the livestock market. In short, he's one of an army of rural entrepreneurs who make the countryside work. Eddie would be the first to admit he couldn't have done it without the support of a great wife, the long-suffering **Clarrie**.

EMMA GRUNDY

(née Carter)

Rickyard Cottage, Brookfield • Born 7.8.84

(Emerald O'Hanrahan)

As she cuddles her beautiful new baby girl, **Keira Susan**, Emma must reflect on how far she has come since leaving husband **Will** to live with his brother **Ed** in a draughty caravan. Along with **George**, her son by Will, they now enjoy the comfort and pleasant surroundings of Rickyard Cottage. Ed's status and income have improved considerably since he became the tenant at **Grange Farm** and took over the small milking herd from **Oliver Sterling**. Emma is able to boost the family income with what she earns cleaning at **Brookfield Farm** and her shift work as a waitress in the Orangery at **Lower Loxley**. Unfortunately, Emma can't resist showing off her new baby to Will and his new partner **Nic**. She knows that any sign of her and Ed doing well upsets Will, who thinks they should be living lives of shame and penury for their treachery. Occasionally, there are glimpses of rapprochement between the two brothers but they seldom last.

GEORGE GRUNDY

Rickyard Cottage, Brookfield / Casa Nueva
Born 7.4.05
(Rui Thacker)

Since his new baby half-sister came along, young George has had a trying time. It's not enough that most of the significant adults in his life seemed to be besotted with the newcomer. He too was expected to carry out tasks to help in the general fuss being made over the new arrival. It's no wonder he threw a few tantrums. Things weren't helped when his father **Will** interpreted his treatment as his brother and ex-wife deliberately favouring their new daughter. Fortunately Grandma **Clarrie** did her best to smooth things over by explaining that the little jobs George had been given were an attempt to get him involved in the circus that must inevitably surround a new baby. Not entirely convinced, Will spends a good deal of time showing George the ropes in the pheasant-rearing pens. The boy is already becoming knowledgeable about the art and science of gamekeeping.

JOE GRUNDY

Keeper's Cottage • Born 18.9.21

(Edward Kelsey)

Joe, the retired farmer, shows no sign of accepting his age and settling down to a life of armchairs and daytime TV. With his grandson **Ed** back as tenant of what used to be the family farm – most of the land anyway – Joe couldn't be happier. He's still very much involved in village affairs – everything from pantos in the Village Hall to the **Ambridge** Bookclub, which he sees as an opportunity to drink free wine and, with his new-found buddie **Jim Lloyd**, generally take the mickey out of the village literati. In fine weather, Joe still gets around on his pony trap with the faithful Bartleby between the shafts. And while active farmwork is now behind him, the former farmer still likes nothing better than to potter about in the field he and son **Eddie** turned into a commercial campsite. The fact that his stock of home-made cider is kept in a container in the same field is pure coincidence.

WILLIAM GRUNDY

Casa Nueva • Born 9.2.83

(Philip Molloy)

Will is a strong believer in natural justice. That's why it gets under his craw to see his ex-wife **Emma** and her partner – his own younger brother **Ed** – apparently doing so well. They have a pleasant cottage. Ed has somehow blagged his way into a farm tenancy that he's sure to make a mess of. And as if it weren't enough that they're bringing up Will's son **George**, they now have a lovely new baby of their own. There's no justice, Will frequently complains to **Nic**, his partner. He's even suggested they should hurry up and have a baby of their own to keep up! It has to be said that Will is happiest when he's with his birds. A countryman through and through, he is now a skilled and thoughtful game-keeper employed by **Borchester Land**. His latest project is to boost the population of native grey partridges on the **Estate**.

Month by month, this once green corner of England grows more like nearby **Grange Farm**, at least the way it looked when the **Grundys** were tenants. Which means it has become a general scrapyard-cum-storage area for various bits of clapped-out farm and construction machinery, bagged compost, garden gnomes and other ornaments. There's a functioning if ageing tractor, a decrepit pole barn and a battered shipping container (which doubles as Eddie's cider store). From time to time, the odd pig or ewe can be seen carefully negotiating its way around the obstacles. At Christmas, there are turkeys in the barn. For **Eddie** and **Joe** this corner of England is the most important place in the world. Social historians might observe that it's in direct line from the English peasantry.

SHIV GUPTA

Coventry

(Shiv Grewal)

Usha Franks's elder brother is an infrequent visitor to **Ambridge**. But Usha knows that whenever she needs family help and support he'll be there for her, as he was when she had a hard time getting her father to accept that she was to marry Church of England vicar **Alan Franks**. Shiv's an accountant by profession. He has a great interest in good food. More than once he's expressed an interest in trying out the restaurant at **Grey Gables** but so far hasn't managed it.

JAKE AND MIA HANSON

Casa Nueva • Born 2004 and 2006

(Charles Thorp and Molly Thorp)

Will **Grundy**'s sadness at not having **George** – his son by ex-wife **Emma** – to live with him was partially alleviated by the arrival of his new partner **Nic**'s youngsters, Jake and Mia. Thanks to their presence, there's a lot more fun and laughter around the keeper's cottage. The two children get on well with their stepbrother **George Grundy**, who spent more time at **Casa Nueva** during the weeks following the arrival of baby **Keira Susan** at Rickyard Cottage.

NICOLA (NIC) HANSON

Casa Nueva • Born 1980

(Becky Wright)

When Nic, along with her two youngsters **Jake** (7) and **Mia** (5), moved in with gamekeeper **Will Grundy**, she was fully aware of the baggage he brought over his former relationship with **Emma**, his ex-wife who now lives with his brother **Ed**. Will's friends would readily admit that Nic brought warmth and laughter to the keeper's cottage. When she was let down by her ex-partner Andrew, Will was all for confronting him. But this was the last thing Nic needed – for Will, the man she loved, to show the same unthinking hostility with which he approached his brother. Will's mother, **Clarrie**, helped him see that his anger stemmed from unresolved hurt over Emma. The realisation came as a shock to Will. But it also seemed to clear away the clutter that was spoiling his relationship with Nic. The two of them are now closer and happier.

PATRICK HENNESSEY

(Joseph Kloska)

Passionate about birds, Patrick works for **Borchester** Wildlife Trust and has a lasting friendship with **Kirsty Miller**, whom he met in **Ambridge Organics**. The two have been on bird-watching trips together, and at her request he has carried out an ornithological survey of the wetland waste water management system at **Bridge Farm**. When asked about their relationship, both Patrick and Kirsty insist that it's mostly about fun and friendship.

HOLLERTON JUNCTION

This pleasant country station continues to enjoy a new lease of life thanks mostly to the growing number of commuters who travel daily from south **Borsetshire** to offices as far away as Birmingham and Worcester. Apart from a brief outbreak of spray-paint graffiti a couple of years ago, the station is kept in pretty good order. And the ticket office is manned for longer hours than it used to be. Recently there have been rumblings of discontent over the rise in car park charges at the station, but generally locals are delighted to have their rail link with the rest of the world. As local resident **Jim Lloyd** pointed out, it's now possible to get an early train at Hollerton and be in Paris for lunch.

NATALIE HOLLINS

Borchester

(Maddie Glasbey)

Jamie Perks's girlfriend – the pair have been going out together since May 2011. While his friends Steve Wilkes and **Marty Bryant** have been bad influences on his life – leading him into petty crime and under-age drinking – Natalie has helped move him in a more positive direction. When Jamie watched his friends steal a car, it was his strong relationship with Natalie that helped him resist getting involved. When Steve and Marty then crashed the car and were subsequently charged, Jamie feared he'd be called upon to be a witness in court. Through it all Natalie proved a wise and loyal friend, helping him to focus on his future in the sixth form. Natalie worked hard at her studies at St Thomas More RC School. She is going to sixth-form college and has been largely instrumental in persuading Jamie to go too.

HOME FARM

STOCK
280 ewes (early lambing) • 110 hinds, stags, calves

CROPS
1,118 acres cereals • 148 acres grassland
158 acres oilseed rape • 36 acres linseed
80 acres woodland • 10 acres willow (game cover)
4 acres strawberries • 6 acres maize
0.5 acres protected cherry trees

OTHER
25-acre riding course • Fishing lake

LABOUR
Adam Macy (managing) • **Debbie Aldridge** (managing)
Andy, Jeff (general workers) • **William Grundy** (gamekeeper)
Pete (assistant keeper) • Students and seasonal labour
Fly (sheepdog)

With 1,585 mainly arable acres, Home Farm is the largest in **Ambridge** and carries out contract work for **Brookfield**, the **Estate** and other local farms. With global commodity prices high, there's great optimism for the future among the team. Manager Adam Macy goes as far as to suggest we may be entering a new golden age for agriculture.

CLIVE HORROBIN

Whereabouts unknown • Born 9.11.72

(Alex Jones)

Clive is the skeleton in the family cupboard as far as **Susan Carter** is concerned. Quite how her family – the **Horrobins** – came to turn out an armed robber, burglar and fire-bomber she finds hard to explain. But he has certainly caused her a lot of pain and anguish. She made the mistake of harbouring him following an armed raid on the village post office, an act of loyalty which earned her a prison sentence. However, following the fire-bombing at the home of former gamekeeper and ex-policeman George Barford, she refused to protect him and he was sentenced to twelve years. He remains a remote but still potent threat to peace and order in **Ambridge**. When **Jennifer Aldridge** arranged a late wedding party for her daughter **Alice** and son-in-law **Christopher**, she was haunted by the thought that Clive – Christopher's uncle – might be allowed out of prison to attend.

THE HORROBINS

6, The Green, and elsewhere

Most residents of **Ambridge** would describe the Horrobins as a 'problem family'. That said, there's plenty of sympathy for the hard-working Ivy, who is heart-broken that her offspring have turned out as they have. Apart from **Susan**, who married pigman **Neil Carter**, they've all become well known to local magistrates. Part of the explanation may lie with their father, Bert. The former council highways worker spent much of his time and most of his money (when he had any) drinking, betting and building up debts. Keith, Gary, Tracy and Stewart – not to mention the infamous **Clive** – grew up with the conviction that proper work was for losers. For whatever reason, Susan seems to have escaped this early conditioning. With her own son **Christopher** now married into a large landowning family – the **Aldridges** – Susan's single-minded devotion to social advance seems to have paid off.

MAURICE HORTON

Borchester

(Philip Fox)

The part-time butcher, who makes **Tom Archer**'s sausages, has a secret weakness – gambling. When he was offered the sausage-making job by Tom, Maurice was already in a lot of trouble. He had lost his wife, his son and one of his businesses through his gambling compulsion. And his second business – a retail shop in **Felpersham** – was also about to go under. Fortunately the offer from Tom came at exactly the right time. With this and other part-time jobs – including the butchering of venison carcasses for **Home Farm** – he was able to pull his life together and get back on his feet. Later Maurice was able to give something back by becoming the sponsor through Gambler's Anonymous for another victim of destructive gambling, vet **Alistair Lloyd**. Hopefully, both are now free of their costly compulsion.

JAXX BAR

Still the coolest venue in **Borchester**, Jaxx has established itself as a favourite among the town's young professionals. This is good news for manager **Kenton Archer** and his backer **Jim Lloyd**. Though the café-bar opened its doors early in the economic downturn, it seems to have weathered the worst of the high-street squalls. With its funky wall art, the bar attracts good numbers during the day and on most nights of the week. These days manager Kenton isn't quite as hands-on as he used to be. He's spending a lot more time at **The Bull** in **Ambridge** with landlady **Jolene Perks**. Having made quite a success of Jaxx, he seems determined to do the same with this popular village pub. However there's some concern among friends that he'll take his eye off the ball at Jaxx and the place will lose some of its popularity. But there's little sign of this happening yet, especially with the popular **Kirsty Miller** running things when Kenton's away.

SATYA KHANNA

Wolverhampton

(Jamila Massey)

Usha Franks's relationship with her Auntie Satya is probably closer than it's ever been. There was a time when Usha viewed her aunt as bossy and interfering. One of the things that annoyed her most was Satya's attempts to become match-maker, suggesting possible marriage partners who were of no interest to Usha. The change in their relationship began when Usha decided to marry **Alan**, a Church of England vicar. At first Satya opposed the match. But when Usha started to feel threatened by the hostility from the Asian community, Satya changed her view and resolutely defended her niece's decision. Nowaday's Usha is always pleased to receive a visit from her aunt. Following the events surrounding the marriage, there is a new respect between the two women. On some issues they will never see eye to eye, but Usha has learned that at times of trouble the ties between them are strong and unbreakable.

ALISTAIR LLOYD

The Stables • Born 1962

(Michael Lumsden)

For vet Alistair, life has become a little more straight forward just lately. First his father **Jim**, who decided to move down from Scotland and settle in **Ambridge**, seems well integrated in village life. In fact, he appears to be more involved in village events than Alistair. Then there's the matter of the education of **Daniel**, his adopted son and child of his wife **Shula**'s first marriage to Mark Hebden. Having been successful in his GCSEs, Daniel seems to have settled down well in the sixth form of **Felpersham** Cathedral School. Having finally kicked into touch his problem gambling (he hopes), Alistair is once again enjoying his life as a rural vet, though he'd be happy spending less time on TB testing. Though the effect of the economic downturn on Shula's equine business continues to cause concern, Alistair is pretty happy with village life. He's captain of the Ambridge cricket team and organises the Single Wicket competition.

DANIEL HEBDEN LLOYD

The Stables • Born 14.11.94

(Louis Hamblett)

The son of **Shula** and her first husband, Mark Hebden, who died in a car crash, Daniel is now in the sixth form at **Felpersham** Cathedral School. To **Alistair Lloyd**, his father by adoption, this wasn't the ideal educational establishment for the boy. But Mark's parents Bunty and Reg are paying for it, so Alistair has gone along with it. Following a good set of GCSE results, Daniel is now getting down to work on his A levels. He has retained his interest in astronomy which stemmed originally from his grandfather Phil's fascination with the subject. Phil's telescope – later bequeathed to Daniel – is now set up in the boy's bedroom. His aim is to become a lawyer like his father and he has spent time on work experience at Jefferson Crabtree, the law firm where **Usha Franks** is a partner.

JIM LLOYD

Greenacres
(John Rowe)

Jim Lloyd's chief pleasure in life is puncturing everything he considers to be pretentious in village life. Since he came to live in **Ambridge**, he's never been short of targets. He's also not averse to playing practical jokes. When **Eddie** and **Joe Grundy** were invited round for a meal at Greenacres, they thought they'd found the solution to **Clarrie**'s proposal of a 'hunger lunch' to raise money during Lent for poor countries. But after the two of them had enjoyed a sumptuous blow-out, Jim cheerfully presented them with a bill, the proceeds to go to the Food Bank. The Ambridge Bookclub has also presented Jim with plenty of mirth-making opportunities. There's a distinct touch of the 'summer wine' about Jim as he drives his breakdown-prone Riley car around the village. His son, vet **Alistair Lloyd**, does his best to ignore the more extreme stunts of his wayward father. Recently he has struck up a charming friendship with **Christine Barford**, who shares his interest in gardening.

SHULA HEBDEN LLOYD

(formerly Hebden, née Archer)
The Stables • Born 8.8.58
(Judy Bennett)

Like all the **Archer** family, Shula has been deeply affected by the rift between her brother **David** and her sister **Elizabeth** following the death of Elizabeth's husband Nigel. She has tried desperately to keep the lines of communication open between the two of them. She was particularly dismayed when Elizabeth asked her to become legal guardian of the twins **Lily** and **Freddie**, should anything happen to their mother. Shula knew David – previously named as guardian in Elizabeth's will – would be hurt by the switch. But Elizabeth insisted she would take responsibility away from David whatever Shula decided. Shula gave in, though she felt terrible about it. The only good thing to come from the situation was that her own rift with **St Stephen's Church** – the result of harsh words following **Alan Franks**'s marriage to a Hindu – had begun to heal. At a trying time for the family, Shula started accompanying her mother **Jill** to the village church once more.

LOWER LOXLEY HALL

The tragic death of Nigel – owner of Lower Loxley – has had major ramifications for all at the minor stately home. For a time Nigel's widow **Elizabeth** tried to keep things going, loyally supported by her brother **David**. But it became clear a full-time manager was needed, and Elizabeth offered the post to **Roy Tucker**, the deputy manager at **Grey Gables**. The appointment was timely, as a deep rift opened up between Elizabeth and David after he confessed to having persuaded Nigel to go up on the roof the night of the accident. The hall's attractions – including conference, wedding and family entertainment centre; treetop walk; rare breeds farm; café, shop and art gallery – are now to be run by Roy, the manager, and Elizabeth. Other staff include ancient retainers Edgar and Eileen Titcombe, **Bert Fry**, a volunteer guide, and **Lorna Gibbs**. **Hayley Tucker** runs activity visits for schoolchildren, and **Emma Grundy** is a waitress in the Orangery.

ADAM MACY

Honeysuckle Cottage • Born 22.6.67

(Andrew Wincott)

Driving one of **Home Farm**'s giant tractors across the fields, Adam must consider himself master of all he surveys. Theoretically, he's joint manager with his half-sister **Debbie** of the 1,585-acre farm along with its contract farming operations. But with Debbie running the family farming interests in Eastern Europe, Adam is mostly left to his own devices. Even his stepfather **Brian Aldridge** – who remains keenly interested in the farm despite handing over the reins to his stepchildren – is now preoccupied with his new career as a developer, having become chairman of **Borchester Land**. Adam gets to make most of the farming decisions that matter, a situation he's more than happy with according to his civil partner, chef **Ian Craig**. So it's come as a shock to learn that Debbie has come up with a proposal for a large-scale livestock enterprise on the **Estate**, land which Adam manages on contract. What hurts most is that he wasn't consulted.

KATE MADIKANE

(née Aldridge)
Johannesburg • Born 30.9.77
(Kellie Bright)

When Kate decided to leave her home in South Africa do a course in development studies at **Felpersham** University, her mother **Jennifer** couldn't help feeling anxious. She remembered too well Kate's restlessness as a teenager when she went to live with a group of travellers, later giving birth to her daughter **Phoebe** in a tepee at the Glastonbury Festival. Phoebe now lives with her father, **Roy Tucker**, stepmother **Hayley** and half-sister **Abbie** in **Ambridge**. Jennifer feared the temporary return of Kate – leaving her other children Noluthando and Sipho with husband **Lucas** in Johannesburg – might unsettle Phoebe. Her worries were confirmed when, encouraged by Kate, Phoebe decided she wanted to spend a year with her real mum in South Africa. Not surprisingly Roy and Hayley weren't thrilled with the idea, but in the end Phoebe's wishes were granted.

LUCAS MADIKANE

Johannesburg • Born 1972

(Connie M'Gadzah)

Kate's marriage to South African Broadcasting Corporation journalist Lucas seems to have been a considerable success as far as her mother **Jennifer** is concerned. At least her once footloose daughter seems to have settled well to family life in Johannesburg. Jennifer suspects that part of the reason must be Lucas's generally easy-going and supportive attitude to Kate's ambitions. So when Kate decided she wanted to complete a course in development studies at **Felpersham** University, Lucas, the hard-working journalist, was nevertheless willing to take over responsibility for their two children. It's true that his parents also played a big part in looking after them during their mother's absence, though Kate visits when she can. But Lucas's agreement was crucial if Kate was to realise her ambitions.

ELONA MAKEPEACE

No 3 The Green
(Eri Shuka)

Elona first came to **Peggy Woolley**'s notice when she worked at the Laurels care home, where **Jack Woolley** is a long-term resident. On her visits to see Jack, who suffers from Alzheimer's, Peggy was impressed by Elona's kindness to residents and families alike. When Peggy learned that Elona – who is married to carpenter Darrell and has two daughters, Ana and Rosa – was thinking of leaving the area, she was determined to help the Albanian-born care assistant. Her efforts weren't made easier when Elona confided in her that husband Darrell was serving a prison term. Peggy has now persuaded her daughter **Lilian** to rent Elona the house she owned – No 3 The Green – and was having difficulty letting. Peggy has also offered the careworker part-time work in her own home, the Lodge.

HARRY MASON

1 Hillside
(Michael Shelford)

In any village popularity contest, Harry the amiable milkman would be pretty well guaranteed to come out in the top five. Chief among his fans would be **Jolene Perks**, landlady of **The Bull**, and her daughter **Fallon Rogers**. In the sad weeks that followed former landlord Sid Perks's death in New Zealand, it was Harry's cheerful support and resourcefulness that helped the pub survive as a business. Just about the only person in **Ambridge** who doesn't view Harry as a paragon is his fellow milkman, the hard-living Glaswegian **Jazzer McCreary**. So it's a mystery to many in Ambridge how the two came to be sharing an apartment together. Whatever the reason, the rivalry between them remains as keen as ever. When Jazzer took a shine to one of the seasonal fruit-pickers at **Home Farm**, Harry felt obliged to save her from becoming just another of the Glaswegian's conquests.

JAZZER McCREARY

1 Hillside • Born 1984

(Ryan Kelly)

In the generally genteel village of **Ambridge**, Jazzer seems to wear his rasping Glaswegian accent and city swagger like a badge of honour. His supposed magnetic appeal to the young women on his milk round sometimes seems to be more in his own imagination than in reality. He certainly came off second best in the contest with fellow-milkman **Harry** for Zofia the strawberry picker. But for all his casual, devil-may-care approach to life, Jazzer has shown himself remarkably loyal to his friends and colleagues. He has stuck with his job delivering milk for **Mike Tucker**, despite the unsocial hours that must play havoc with his social life. And his commitment to the pigs at **Bridge Farm**, where he works part-time, has impressed everyone, not least farmer **Tom Archer**. Though no one would risk saying it to his face, there's a softness to Jazzer's character that isn't entirely masked by his bravado.

KIRSTY MILLER

Borchester

(Anabelle Dowler)

Ever since **Helen Archer** – owner of **Ambridge Organics** – had her baby, assistant Kirsty has been taking on more and more responsibility for the day-to-day running of the shop. And Helen would be the first to admit that she's done a pretty good job – this at a time when the economic downturn has made life pretty tough for organic businesses. Kirsty also works part-time in the popular **Jaxx** café-bar. Perhaps because of her busy work life, her social life is not quite as upbeat as she'd like. The friendship with birder and wildlife trust worker **Patrick Hennessey**, while warm and enjoyable, continues to be just that – a friendship. However it's a friendship that seems to take up more of their time as they go bird-watching and take part in conservation volunteer events.

PAUL MORGAN

(Michael Fenton Stevens)

Lilian Bellamy can't quite forget Paul, her partner **Matt Crawford**'s half-brother, who turned up unexpectedly at the Dower House while Matt was serving a prison sentence for fraud. The purpose of Paul's visit was to persuade Matt to visit his sick mother before she died. What he hadn't expected was that he'd feel an immediate attraction to Lilian, a feeling that was mutual. In the event Lilian's love for Matt was too strong, and she drew back from the passionate affair that for a brief moment beckoned. But she still can't quite forget the feeling and the man who induced it.

ELIZABETH PARGETTER

(née Archer)

Lower Loxley Hall • Born 21.4.67

(Alison Dowling)

The tragic death of Nigel, her beloved husband, brought out the best – and sometimes the worst – in Elizabeth. The shock of the events in January could have led to a complete breakdown. But the young widow knew she had to be strong for the twins, **Lily** and **Freddie**, and also for Nigel, to whom **Lower Loxley**, the family home and estate, meant everything. Determined to hold the business together, she threw herself into the task of running the multi-faceted estate, taking full advantage of her brother **David**'s unstinting offer of help. Gratitude turned to condemnation, however, when she discovered David's role in the accident. Her bitter resentment of her brother brought anguish to the whole family. Following a heart operation, Elizabeth now relies on new manager **Roy Tucker** to help her run Lower Loxley. Those closest to her hope she'll be able to come to terms with her loss rather than blaming it all on David.

LILY AND FREDDIE PARGETTER

Lower Loxley Hall • Born 12.12.99

(Georgie Feller and Jack Firth)

Coming to terms with the death of their father has been a painful process in the young lives of Lily and Freddie. Their courage and fortitude in meeting this cruel challenge has helped their mother **Elizabeth** to cope. As if this weren't enough of a challenge for the youngsters, they've had to adjust to life in senior school, something Lily achieved quickly but which was a little more traumatic for her brother. Through it all, the youngsters have remained brave and resolute. Their father Nigel would have been very proud of them. Freddie has a lot of Nigel in him – he's keen on horses and the hunt, and often visits **the Stables** where Nigel's old horse Topper is liveried. Both Freddie and Lily enjoy Pony Club events.

JAMIE PERKS

April Cottage • Born 20.7.95

(Dan Ciotkowski)

Jamie's life began to disintegrate with the death of his father, the popular landlord of **The Bull**, Sid Perks. For a while Jamie sought consolation with his mother **Kathy**'s then boyfriend, **Kenton Archer**. But when the relationship broke up, Jamie's life began to spiral into drinking and petty vandalism. As his relationship with his mother broke down, Jamie spent more time at the pub, moving in and getting a part-time job. With support from his girlfriend, **Natalie**, he seemed more settled. Kathy was relieved when he sat his GCSEs. But with his friends **Marty** and Steve he became involved in a round of petty theft culminating in car theft. Later he witnessed a car smash involving his two friends. It was a traumatic experience but his loyal girlfriend – plus a closer relationship with Kenton – helped him get through. He has now moved back home and is going to sixth form college. Kathy remains hopeful about his future.

JOLENE PERKS

(née Rogers)
The Bull
(Buffy Davis)

The death of her husband, popular publican Sid Perks, came as a severe blow to the normally happy-go-lucky Jolene. **The Bull**, which had become her life, suddenly didn't seem a good place to be. She even considered selling up, a course of action opposed by her daughter **Fallon Rogers**, who helped keep the business viable. The situation was transformed when Jolene – against all her expectations – began a relationship with **Kenton Archer**, who ran **Jaxx** café-bar in **Borchester**. With Kenton at her side, Jolene became interested in the pub again. She was delighted when he offered to take over the catering side of the business, persuading cook **Freda Fry** to be more adventurous in the kitchen. Thanks to Jolene's new-found happiness, the village pub is a good place to be again. She remains concerned about Sid's son **Jamie**. She also retains contact with former husband and country singer Wayne Tucson, who lives in Borchester.

KATHY PERKS

(formerly Holland)
April Cottage • Born 30.1.53
(Hedli Niklaus)

Kathy's recent life has been blighted by damaged relationships. Following the death of her ex-husband Sid, which affected her deeply, she broke up with her boyfriend **Kenton Archer**. The break-up put a further strain on her deteriorating relationship with her son **Jamie**. He had grown close to Kenton following his father's death, and he blamed his mother for the break-up. Kathy grew increasingly concerned about Jamie as he became involved in vandalism and drinking with his friends **Marty** and Steve. She was shocked to learn that the two had been involved in a smash in a stolen car and Jamie had been a witness. The event seemed to bring Jamie to his senses. Kathy was relieved that his GCSE results were better than he had expected and that he was going to the sixth form college. She also realised that his girlfriend **Natalie Hollins** was having a good influence on him. Kathy was supported through her tribulations by her friend **Pat Archer**.

HEATHER PRITCHARD

Prudhoe, Northumberland
(Joyce Gibbs)

Though she enjoys an active social life in her home town of Prudhoe, **Ruth Archer**'s mum greatly looks forward to her occasional visits to **Ambridge** to see her grandchildren, **Pip**, **Josh** and **Ben**. Whenever she's in the village she takes the opportunity to visit the old friends she has made over the years. Among her favourites are vet **Alistair Lloyd**'s father **Jim**. She was very fond of Phil and his death came as a shock.

FALLON ROGERS

The Bull • Born 19.6.85

(Joanna van Kampen)

No one is more relieved that pub landlady **Jolene Perks** is once more happy running the place than her daughter Fallon. When it began to look as if the pub might close, Fallon and her good friend **Harry Mason** played a key role in keeping it going. Fallon's own career as singer in the band Little White Lies has been slow of late, which means she has more time to promote events at the popular pub venue 'Upstairs@The Bull'. Initially amused to see Harry and his fellow milkman **Jazzer McCreary** competing for the attentions of strawberry-picker Zofia, she felt a little sad when Harry clearly won the day – and the girl's heart. She watched from the sidelines as the romance progressed until it was time for Zofia to return to her home country. Harry being 'just a friend', he was, of course, perfectly at liberty to go out with whoever he liked.

GRAHAM RYDER

Borchester
(Malcolm McKee)

Graham used to be a regular visitor to **Ambridge**. That was in the days when this busy land agent, who works for the **Borchester** firm of Rodways, had an office on the **Estate**, now owned by **Borchester Land**. **Matt Crawford**, then chair of the company, passed the land management responsibility to **Debbie Aldridge**, so the services of Rodways are no longer required. Graham spends most of his time looking after farms and estates elsewhere in **Borsetshire**, including **Lower Loxley**. When he does visit the village, it's usually to check up on the annual pantomime in the Village Hall.

ANNABELLE SCHRIVENER

Felpersham

(Julia Hills)

At the time when **Brian Aldridge** was involved in a boardroom battle for control of the development company **Borchester Land**, he viewed Annabelle, senior partner of a law firm specialising in property, as a key ally. So when it came to setting up a board to run the new livestock market, Brian at once thought of her. However, following a few fractious meetings of the new board – **Borchester** Market Developments – Brian has discovered that he can't automatically depend on her support. She certainly shares his ambition to take the parent company, BL, into the big league of regional developers. But it's clear the woman with the formidable legal mind and the ability to charm any opposition is very much her own person. Annabelle's competitive streak shows through even in her leisure activities. She likes to run and is a keen competitor in the Felpersham Marathon.

SILENT CHARACTERS

These are the extras in the great pageant that is **Ambridge** life. They've pulled off the not inconsiderable feat of stamping their personalities on the village without their voices having been heard. The current crop includes Reg Hebden, the father of **Shula**'s late husband Mark; Mrs Potter and Mr Pullen of Manorfield Close; the Titcombes – Edgar and Eileen – who are gardener and housekeeper at **Lower Loxley**; Jessica, Lower Loxley's resident falconer; Pete, the under-keeper on the **Estate** shoot; **Home Farm** staff Andy and Jeff; **Eddie Grundy**'s friends Baggy and Fat Paul; bell-ringer Neville Booth and his nephew Nathan; Leigh Barham, director of golf at **Ambridge Golf Club**; Richard and Sabrina Thwaite; the Buttons; Derek Fletcher, former chair of the Parish Council and village busybody; a number of **Horrobins**; the ever popular cook at **The Bull**, **Freda Fry**; and Rosemary Hopwood, **Lily** and **Freddie**'s private tutor at Lower Loxley.

CORIANDER AND LEONIE SNELL

Born 1974 and 1975

(Alexandra Lilley and Sara Poyzer)

Occasional visits from **Robert Snell**'s two daughters by his first marriage seem to cause much excitement in the Snell household. Coriander, known as 'Caz', had a baby boy – Oscar – in 2009, giving much delight to Robert and 'step-grandma' **Lynda**. More recently, the appearance of Leonie with **Lilian Bellamy**'s son **James** has given both families a good deal to think about.

LYNDA SNELL

Ambridge Hall • Born 29.5.47

(Carole Boyd)

It's hard to believe that Lynda has been in **Ambridge** for only twenty-five years. You feel she must have been there for ever. But no, it's twenty-five years, and Lynda felt it should be celebrated. She and husband **Robert** would throw a party to mark their Silver Anniversary in Ambridge. You might think she had enough on her plate already. She's senior receptionist at **Grey Gables** hotel, and with Robert runs a B&B enterprise at **Ambridge Hall**. Then there's the little matter of being a volunteer in the **Ambridge Community Shop**, plus of course the production of the annual village panto. Her highlight of the year was surely her chance encounter with the Duchess of Cornwall during the royal visit to Grey Gables. Unfortunately, Lynda missed seeing her during the official proceedings. But luckily she was replacing the chain of her bicycle at the bottom of Grey Gables drive when the royal car swept by and Lynda received a special wave.

ROBERT SNELL

Ambridge Hall • Born 5.4.43

(Graham Blockey)

Robert used to run his own software business. Now he has become **Ambridge**'s resident handyman while pretty much devoting his life to supporting his wife **Lynda**'s projects. This included helping her arrange and run the summer party to celebrate their twenty-five years in Ambridge. At home in **Ambridge Hall**, he's the chief greeter and cook in the B&B enterprise. He has two daughters from a first marriage – **Leonie** and **Coriander**, who has given him a baby grandson, Oscar. Leonie surprised him when she started going out with **James Bellamy**, the son of **Lilian**. Robert is very fond of cricket and as yet shows no sign of giving up the sport.

ST STEPHEN'S CHURCH

Consecrated 1281

Over the centuries, this beautiful church has provided habitats for many wild species. The current crop includes bats in the tower and stag beetles in the churchyard. But until now it has never been home to a peregrine falcon, at least, not as far as any village residents can remember. **Lynda Snell** was delighted to discover that peregrines were nesting on the church tower. She came up with a proposal to encourage further nesting by putting up a special ledge for them on the east side of the tower. Unfortunately the plan encountered stiff opposition in the village. Among those opposing the plan were **Peggy Woolley**, **Brian Aldridge**, **Susan Carter** and gamekeeper **Will Grundy**. In the end the Parish Council voted against Lynda's proposal. However, she found some consolation in the return of the peregrines to nest on St Stephen's the following year – even without her ledge.

THE STABLES

Business has picked up slightly following the economic downturn. This has come as a great relief to owner **Shula Hebden Lloyd** and her husband **Alistair Lloyd**. Shula bought the Stables from her aunt, **Christine Barford**, back in 2001. Like other independent traders, the business was dealt a painful blow by the recession, forcing Shula to economise on the use of casual staff. She and Alistair were glad to have his earnings as a vet to provide them with a steady income. However, there are signs that equestrian businesses have started to pick up, and Shula is hoping for a better year.

CAROLINE STERLING

(née Bone, formerly Pemberton)

Grange Farm • Born 3.4.55

(Sara Coward)

With her husband **Oliver**, Caroline bought the up-market country hotel that she had spent much of her life managing. However, she'd have to acknowledge that her timing wasn't perfect. She ended up buying the place just as the economic downturn was beginning to bite. Though they haven't been hit as hard as many in the hotel business, income has taken something of a nosedive in recent months. Shocked as she was to be told by deputy manager **Roy Tucker** that he wished to give his notice in as he'd been offered a job at **Lower Loxley**, she saw it could be a cost-saving exercise. For the time being she decided to manage without a manager and do the job herself. It meant working harder and for longer hours than before, she told Oliver, but she was sure it would work out in the end. Oliver wasn't entirely convinced.

OLIVER STERLING

Grange Farm
(Michael Cochrane)

When Oliver decided to rent out his small farm and sell its herd of Guernsey cows to cowman **Ed Grundy**, his plan was to have more time to spend socially with his wife **Caroline**. Unfortunately, it hasn't quite worked out like that. With Caroline's hotel business suffering from the economic downturn, she decided not to replace general manager **Roy Tucker** when he took the job of managing the events business at **Lower Loxley**. Caroline told Oliver that for a trial period of six months she would try running **Grey Gables** herself. Suddenly finding himself at a loose end when his wife was busier than ever, Oliver looked around for something to do. He spent more time at the hunt kennels and even agreed to do some relief milking on his former dairy herd. He also spends time in the **Ambridge Community Shop** as one of the volunteer team leaders. But what he'd most like to be doing is spending more time with Caroline.

MABEL THOMPSON

Bradford

(Mona Hammond)

The mother of vicar **Alan Franks**'s deceased first wife Catherine, Mabel doesn't make many visits to **Ambridge** these days. But Alan speaks to her regularly on the phone, and he's glad of her advice and encouragement whenever he's taxed about any particular issue. Mabel is a woman of strong Christian principles and is an active member of her local evangelical church. After some initial difficulties of conscience, she has now fully accepted Alan's marriage to Hindu **Usha Gupta**. She sees it as her duty to support Alan in his ministry, and if that includes accepting Usha as the vicar's wife, she is prepared to go along with it. However, Mabel's occasional visits to Ambridge continue to be lively and challenging.

ABIGAIL (ABBIE) TUCKER

Willow Farm • Born 7.3.08

(Daisy Pettifer)

Abbie is the first child of **Hayley** and **Roy Tucker**. The three of them live with **Phoebe Aldridge**, the daughter of Roy Tucker and **Kate Madikane**, now back in Johannesburg after taking a course at **Felpersham** University. Abbie is an amiable child with a particular attachment to **Mike Tucker**'s second wife **Vicky**, which is baffling to some members of the family.

BRENDA TUCKER

1 The Green • Born 21.1.81

(Amy Shindler)

After graduating in marketing at **Felpersham** University, Brenda took a job with a marketing agency in Leicester, a job requiring a long and tiring commute. She now works as PA to property developers **Lilian Bellamy** and **Matt Crawford**. Her partner **Tom**'s not entirely happy about this. For a long time he pressed her for a wedding date, which Brenda interpreted as 'Come back home and let's start a family.' Brenda was in no great hurry to have children. And following the financial meltdown at **Bridge Farm**, the result of the E. coli outbreak, she wasn't at all sure that giving up her independent income would be a very sensible move. Tom could see the sense of her argument. He stopped all talk of wedding dates and concentrated on getting the farm back on its feet.

HAYLEY TUCKER

(née Jordan)
Willow Farm • Born 1.5.77
(Lorraine Coady)

Hayley must wonder if her little family will ever be free of the disruptive influence of her husband **Roy**'s first partner, **Kate Madikane**. Hayley works at **Lower Loxley Hall**, where she runs activities for visiting school parties. She is also mother to **Phoebe** – husband Roy's daughter by Kate – and **Abbie**, the happy result of her own struggle to become pregnant. The family live in the house Roy grew up in – the farmhouse at **Willow Farm**. Next door Roy's father **Mike** lives with his new wife **Vicky**. With Roy in a challenging new job at Lower Loxley, the future's looking bright. The only cloud on the horizon was Kate's return from South Africa to do a course at **Felpersham**. Encouraged by her mum, Phoebe decided that she wanted to spend a year in South Africa living with her mother. Despite opposition from Roy and Hayley, Phoebe got her way and is now spending the year there.

MIKE TUCKER

Willow Cottage • Born 1.12.49

(Terry Molloy)

Mike's whirlwind romance so soon after the death of his first wife Betty didn't go down well with all the family. Mike's daughter **Brenda** in particular found it hard to take to **Vicky**, the new Mrs Tucker. But with the couple clearly head-over-heels in love with each other, Brenda just had to go along with it. These days, Mike's marriage is a little less spectacular, but his new-found happiness has given him a fresh enthusiasm for his varied working life. Despite the continued rise in supermarket milk sales, his local milk rounds continue to flourish, in part because of the popularity of **Ed Grundy**'s mainly pasture-fed milk. Mike also finds time to look after the Millennium Wood, which now requires regular coppicing. When tragedy struck at **Lower Loxley Hall**, Mike was on hand to do his bit to help the grieving **Elizabeth** by quietly cutting back the laurels. Only at **David Archer**'s insistence did he put in an invoice for the work. He was quite prepared to make the work his gift to the sorrowing Elizabeth.

ROY TUCKER

Willow Farm • Born 2.2.78

(Ian Pepperell)

Having been a successful deputy manager at **Grey Gables**, Roy has now taken the job of manager at **Lower Loxley Hall**, where he'll be running the conference and events business along with owner **Elizabeth**. It's an exciting new challenge for Roy, but giving in his notice at Grey Gables was hard, given the support and encouragement he'd received from owner **Caroline Sterling** over the years. However, Roy – husband of the warm and effervescent **Hayley**, and father of their daughter **Abbie** and of **Phoebe**, his child with **Kate Madikane**, formerly Aldridge – is now looking to the future. The family live in half of the farmhouse at **Willow Farm**, next door to his father **Mike** and his second wife, **Vicky**. For a lad who was once part of a racist gang that terrorised Asian lawyer **Usha Franks** (née Gupta), Roy has matured and made quite a success of his life.

VICKY TUCKER

(née Hudson)

Willow Cottage

(Rachel Atkins)

Following her whirlwind romance with **Mike Tucker**, Vicky hit **Ambridge** like a hurricane. Not only did she have her new husband flinging off his clothes on a nude beach near their honeymoon hotel, she quickly set out to make her mark on rural life. Having invested in **Ed Grundy**'s dairy herd, she wanted to get involved in their management. When Ed didn't particularly welcome her intervention, she naturally felt hurt. But in family matters Vicky's thoughtful contributions have been more welcome. When **Phoebe Aldridge** decided she wanted to spend a year in South Africa with **Kate Madikane**, her birth mother, her adopted mum – **Hayley** – felt upset and hurt. While sympathising with Hayley, Vicky gently pointed out that Phoebe's wish to spend time with Kate was entirely natural, and that by blocking it Hayley ran the risk of alienating her daughter. It was wise counsel from the older woman that Hayley later appreciated.

UNDERWOODS

Well Street, Borchester

These are not good times on the high streets of Britain, and **Borchester**'s own department store is struggling to weather the downturn. Even the Food Hall and coffee shop – once the jewels in the crown – have been experiencing lean times just lately. They were not helped by an E. coli outbreak that was tracked down to **Bridge Farm** dairy products, a brand the store has featured for years. The affected products were quickly cleared from the shelves, and the store is optimistic that sales will quickly recover. And the coffee shop continues to be a better source of local news than the *Borchester Echo* and Radio Borsetshire combined.

SPENCER WILKES

(Johnny Venkman)

The boyfriend of **Pip Archer**, Spencer lives on an arable farm between Lakey Green and **Lower Loxley**. After getting a degree in agriculture, he went back home to work on the family farm, where he's chiefly interested in using new technologies such as precision farming to reduce the farm's carbon footprint. At home the bane of his life is younger brother Steve, who has little interest in farming and whose main occupation seems to be getting into trouble. Spencer met Pip at the local branch of the Young Farmers Club. Pip's parents **David** and **Ruth** took to him immediately. This may be partly because he's a fellow farmer. But it might have something to do with the fact that her previous boyfriend was the much older and (to them) totally unsuitable Jude.

RHYS WILLIAMS

Over the village shop

(Scott Arthur)

Originally from South Wales, the popular barman in **The Bull** is known for being something of a wind-up merchant. But even when he's pulling your leg it's hard to take offence from the cheerful Rhys. He was an instant hit with **Peggy Woolley**, which is the main reason he's now tenant of the flat over the village shop, which she owns. Now living at the heart of the village, Rhys keeps a pretty close eye on what goes on. A good deal of it is then incorporated into witty stories passed over the bar of The Bull.

WILLOW FARM

The farmhouse is split into two homes. On one side, **Roy Tucker** lives with his wife **Hayley** and daughters **Phoebe** and **Abbie**. There's a good bit of fun and laughter from this side of the house. On the other side, **Mike Tucker** lives with his wife **Vicky** amid the bright décor she chose to match the spirit of their marriage. Nearby are eight acres owned by **Neil Carter**. Neil and his wife **Susan** live in their own self-built house, while alongside is the land where Neil runs his outdoor herd of breeding sows. There's also an organic free-range laying bird enterprise run by Neil in partnership with Hayley Tucker.

HAZEL WOOLLEY

LA, New York, Tooting… who knows?

Born 15.2.56

(Annette Badland)

Hazel is **Jack Woolley**'s adopted daughter. She claims to be a film director, though there is no evidence of this. She rarely appears in **Ambridge** now Jack is in a nursing home suffering from advanced dementia. Hazel has never got on particularly well with Jack's wife **Peggy**, who was convinced her only interest in her father lay in working out ways of getting hold of his money.

JACK WOOLLEY

The Lodge, Grey Gables • Born 19.7.19

(Arnold Peters)

Jack used to be **Ambridge**'s most successful businessman. The self-made Brummie, who once owned **Grey Gables**, the country park and golf course, along with the ***Borchester*** *Echo* newspaper, now lives in the Laurels, a nursing home, where he is cared for as he suffers from Alzheimer's. His devoted (third) wife **Peggy** looks after his business and financial affairs, visiting him regularly. She rarely gets much response from him these days. Nevertheless her love for him remains undimmed.

PEGGY WOOLLEY

(née Perkins, formerly Archer)
The Lodge, Grey Gables • Born 13.11.24
(June Spencer)

As Peggy sits with her beloved husband **Jack**, she sometimes reflects upon her long life in **Ambridge**. The East End girl who lived through the Blitz has had her share of troubles since arriving in the village. Her first husband – also Jack – was at one time landlord of **The Bull**. He was also an alcoholic, which made life difficult for them both. Now, as she watches the man she has loved for many years slowly leave her, she must work out how she will live life without him. Through it all, her comfort is the family – her children, **Jennifer Aldridge**, **Lilian Bellamy** and **Tony Archer**, plus the various grandchildren. To all of them Peggy is a rock – solid, dependable and always ready to help in any way she can.

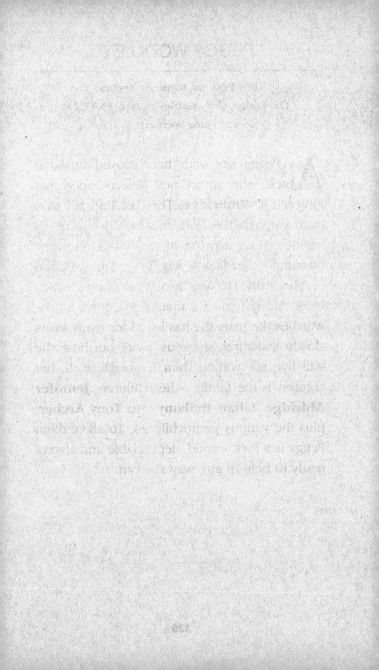